Snake & Ladder [A Creation of Niyati Programming - Design & Code: Anurag Pandey - Em

Turn ON Ur Own Dice

STOP MOV.
LADDERS!!

TURN ON AUTO
PLAY

Value of (PLAYER 2
???): 6 + 3

Dear beginners, learners and students, develop your own VB Based Gaming Application in just 1-2 hours

Code & Design of VB Based Game Snake & Ladder (With 2 Auto Moving Ladders)

PLAYER
THE DICE!

PLAYER 1 ???

PLAYER

Step by step guide with complete design, complete code along with all required Images.

Author, Design & Code: Anurag Pandey

Min :Set Pause between : Max
ENTER

Develop your own VB Based Gaming Application just in hours

Code & Design of VB Based Game Snake & Ladder (With 2 Auto Moving Ladders)

Step by step guide with complete design, complete code along with all required Images.

With help of this book Visual Basic beginners, learners and students anyone can develop Snake & Ladder gaming application in just 1 or 2 hours by following the design guide and given code.

Author Design & Code: Anurag S Pandey

Dear Friends,

If you are Visual Basic beginner, learner, student or programmer, this book will be helpful to you. Using design support and Complete CODE given in this book, you will be able to develop your own Snake & Ladder VB Based Gaming Application just in one or two hours. This application will have two auto moving ladders, which shall dramatically send the player up as well as down. However Design and CODE are complete and need no modification, but you can also improvise the design and CODE as per your wish. If you are beginner then this book will help you a lot to understand Visual Basic Coding, Applying Logics and Methods into programs etc.

It is understood that you are at least little familiar with Visual Basic and you have Visual Basic installed on your PC.

So we shall now develop our VB based Snake & Ladder gaming application step by step:

Step 1:

Open Visual Basic and create New Project.

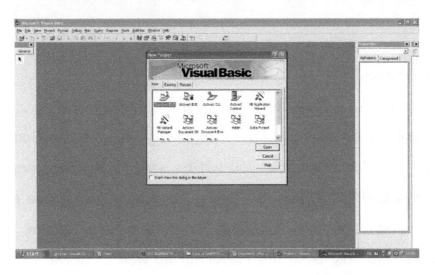

Step 2:

Save Form1.frm

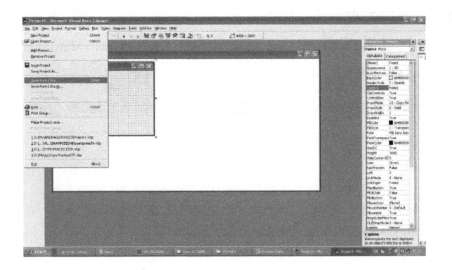

Step 3:

Name it or let it be default "Form1"

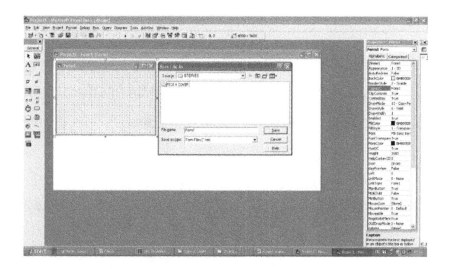

Step 4:

Save Project the same way

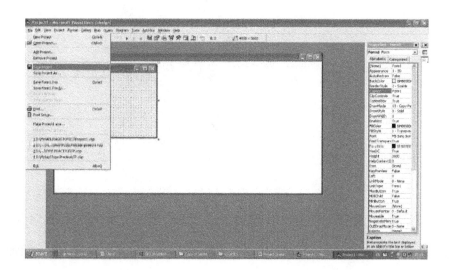

Step 5:

Using Copy and Paste in to MSPaint or using Scan save each of below pictures into separate jpg files.

Image 1: SNAKE-BACKGROUND.jpg [It will be used as Background image of VB Form1. Logic of Game is linked with boxes drawn on this image, so you have to use this image only.]

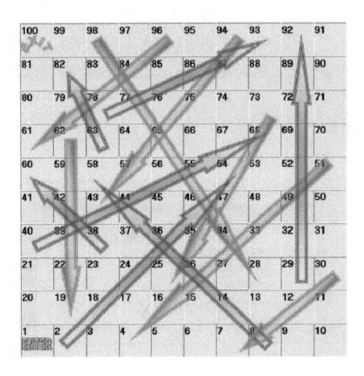

IMPORTANT ABOUT BACKGROUND IMAGE: Save this image with any name.jpg or background.jpg. This image Pixels must be

825 Width X 660 Height. So you have to resize this picture with help of some app or do like this. Open this Image with Microsoft Office Picture Manager - Click on Edit Pictures - Click on Resize - Select Custom Width X Height – Enter Width = 825 and Height = 660 – Click on OK – Save the Image. DONE. We don't need to resize other images.

Image 2: PAASE1.JPG [It will be used as Picture of Image1(0)]

Image 3: PAASE2.JPG [It will be used as Picture of Image1(1)]

Image 4: PAASE3.JPG [It will be used as Picture of Image1(2)]

Image 5: PAASE4.JPG [It will be used as Picture of Image1(3)]

Image 6: PAASE5.JPG [It will be used as Picture of Image1(4)]

Image 7: PAASE6.JPG [It will be used as Picture of Image1(5)]

Image 8: Cone1.jpg [It will be used as Picture of Image2(0)]

Image 9: Cone2.jpg [It will be used as Picture of Image2(1)]

Image 10: Button.jpg [It will be used as Picture of Command Button Command1(0)]

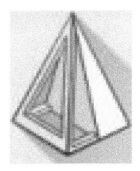

Step 6:

Now we have to design our VB Form like below.

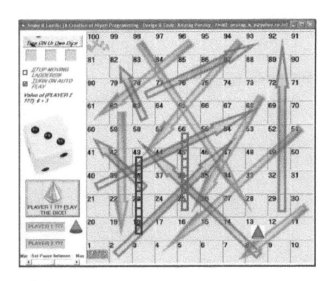

Confused?

Let me clear you.

Here looks your Form1 now.

Set Form1 width = 12525

Set Form1 height = 10500

Set Form1 StartUpPosition = 2- CenterScreen

Now your Form1 looks like this.

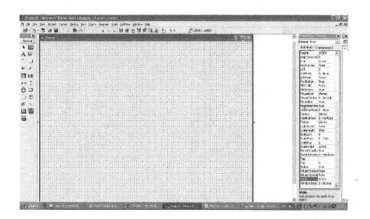

Now Set Form1 Picture = SNAKE-BACKGROUND.jpg image

First set the background image to the form. Then your Form1 would look like below.

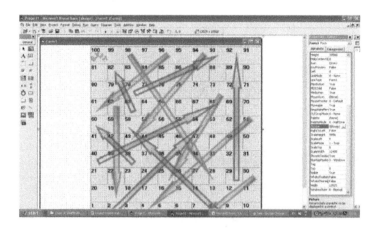

Now we shall add following controls one by one.

First of all we shall add Array of Command Buttons. There are two Command Buttons – Command1(0) and Command1(1)

PLAY THE DICE is an array of command button Command1. Name it Command1(0).

Set Command1(0) Top = 6360

Set Command1(0) Left = 240

Set Command1(0) Height = 1575

Set Command1(0) Width = 2295

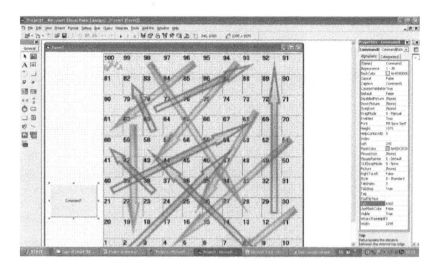

Set Command1(0) Caption = "&PLAY THE DICE"

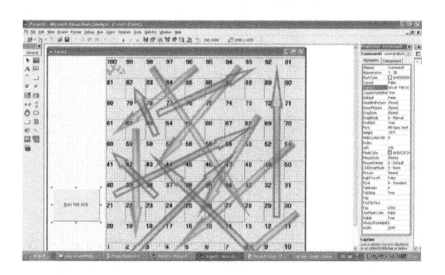

Set Command1(0) Backcolor = &H0080FF80&

Set Command1(0) Style = 1 – Graphical

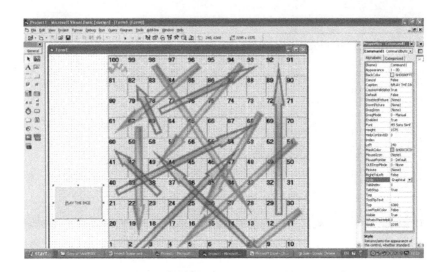

Set Command1(0) Picture = Button.jpg image

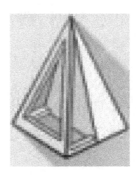

Now Form1 would look like this

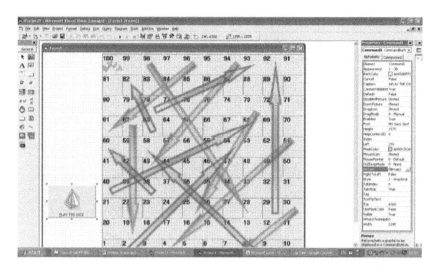

Now we shall add Command1(1). At present Command1(0) Name is "Command1". Now we shall make array of this. Select Command1, then RIGHT CLICK then COPY. Then Paste.

A Message Box will appear – You already have a control named "Command1". Do you want to create a control array?

Click on YES. Now you have two Command buttons – Commaqnd1(0) and Command1(1) like below.

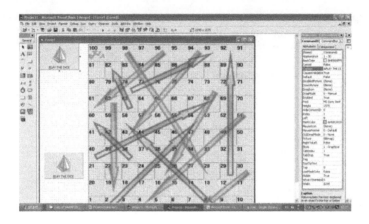

Set Command1(1) Caption = "Turn ON Ur &Own Dice"

Set Command1(1) Top = 240

Set Command1(1) Left = 120

Set Command1(1) Height = 495

Set Command1(1) Width = 2535

You can set Command1(1) Picture of your choice. Now Form1 would look like this.

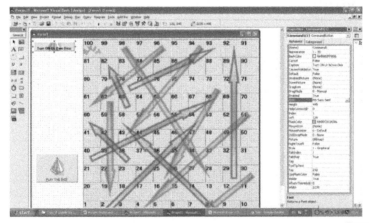

Now we shall add Image Control.

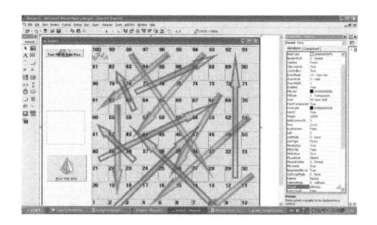

Set Image1(0) Top = 3600

Set Image1(0) left = 120

Set Image1(0) Height = 2745

Set Image1(0) Width = 2370

Set Image1(0) Visible = False

Set Image1(0) Picture = Passe1.jpg

Now Form1 would look like this

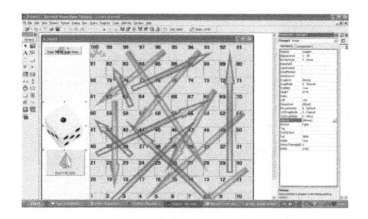

Now we shall create array of Image control the same way we had created array of Command Button.

Select Image Control then RIGHT CLICK then COPY then PASTE then CLICK on YES.

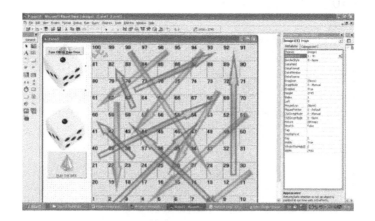

Repeat this until you get total SIX IMAGE Controls. They will have names Image1(0), Image1(1), Image1(2), Image1(3), Image1(4) and Image1(5).

Set Image1(1) Picture = Paase2.jpg

Set Image1(2) Picture = Paase3.jpg

Set Image1(3) Picture = Paase4.jpg

Set Image1(4) Picture = Paase5.jpg

Set Image1(5) Picture = Paase6.jpg

Now form1 would look like below.

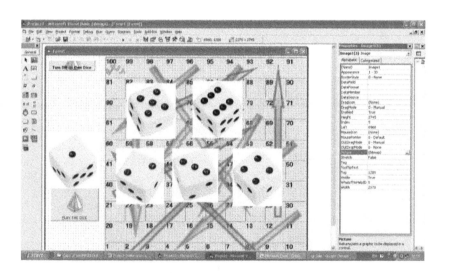

Now set Top and Left of all Image same to Image1(0). Now your Form1 would look like below.

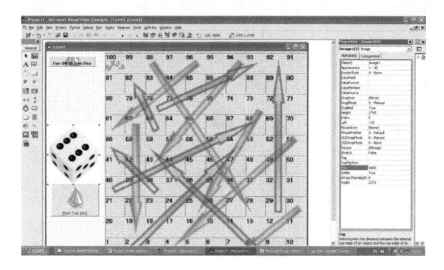

Now we shall add Textbox Control like below

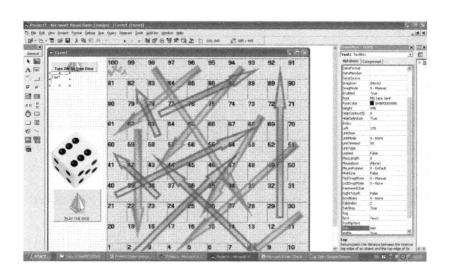

Set Text1 Text = ""

Set Text1 Enabled = FALSE

Set Text1 Height = 495

Set Text1 Width = 495

Set Text1 Top = 840

Set Text1 Left = 240

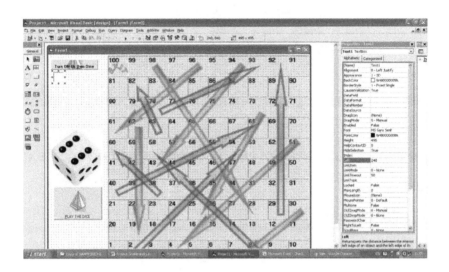

Now create array of Textbox. Create three Textboxes, Text1(0),

Text1(1) and Text1(2) like below

Set Text1(1) Left = 1080

Set Text1(2) Left = 1920

Now Form1 would look like this.

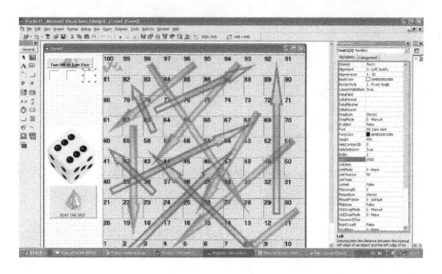

Now we shall create Array of two Textbox the same way, Text2(0) and Text2(1).

Text2(0) Top = 8160

Text2(0) Left = 240

Text2(0) Height = 420

Text2(0) Width = 1695

Text2(0) Text = "PLAYER 1 ???"

Text2(1) Top = 8880

Text2(1) Left = 240

Text2(1) Height = 420

Text2(1) Width = 1695

Text2(1) Text = "PLAYER 2 ???"

Now your Form1 would look like this

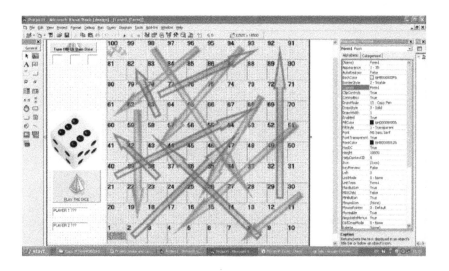

Now we shall add Array of another Image Control – Image2(0) and Image2(1) like below

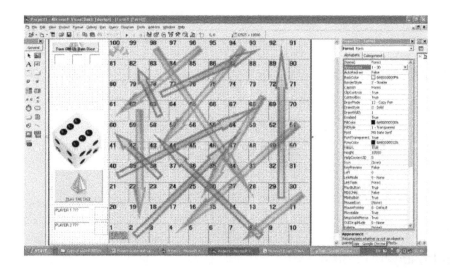

Set Image2(0) Picture = Cone1.jpg

Set Image2(1) Picture = Cone2.jpg

Set Image2(0) Top = 8040

Set Image2(0) Left = 2100

Set Image2(0) Height = 615

Set Image2(0) Width = 555

Set Image2(0) Stretch = True

Set Image2(1) Top = 8760

Set Image2(1) Left = 2100

Set Image2(1) Height = 645

Set Image2(1) Width = 570

Set Image2(1) Stretch = True

Now Form1 would look like below.

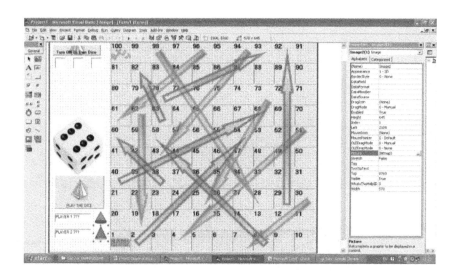

Now Add Label Control named Label1(0) below with below properties

Label1(0). Caption = "Min :Set Pause between : Max"

Label1(0) Top = 9480

Label1(0) Left = 0

Label1(0) Height = 195

Label1(0) Width = 2730

Label1(0) BackStyle = 0- Transparent

Now Form1 would look like below:

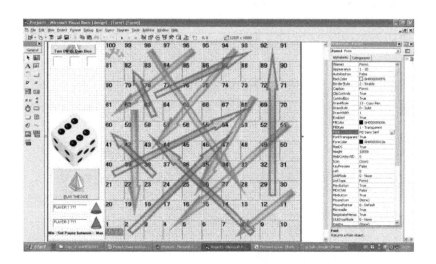

Same way add Label1(1) with properties like below

Label1(1). Caption = "Value :"

Label1(1) Top = 2640

Label1(1) Left = 120

Label1(1) Height = 615

Label1(1) Width = 2415

Label1(1) BackStyle = 0- Transparent

Now Form1 would look like below:

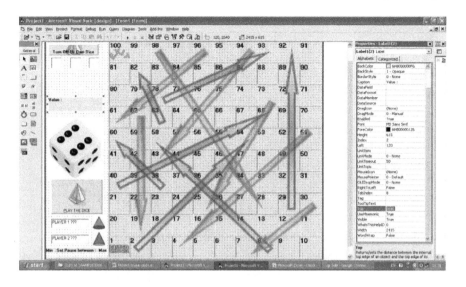

BackStyle property of Label1(0) and Label1(1) are set later as Transparent. Now same way we shall add Label1(2) with properties like below:

Label1(2). Caption = ""

Label1(2) BackColor = &H00FFFFC0&

Label1(2) Top = 2040

Label1(2) Left = 4680

Label1(2) Height = 5895

Label1(2) Width = 6615

Label1(2) Visible = FALSE

Now Form1 would look like this

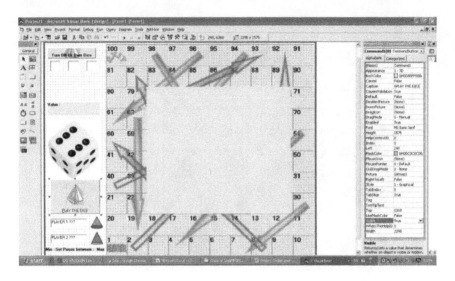

Now we shall add two Checkboxes

Check1 and Check2 with below properties

Check1 Caption = "&TURN ON AUTO PLAY"

Check1 Top = 2040

Check1 Left = 120

Check1 Height = 495

Check1 Width = 2415

Check1 BackColor = &H80000005&

Check2 Caption = "&STOP MOVING LADDERS!!!"

Check2 Top = 1560

Check2 Left = 120

Check2 Height = 495

Check2 Width = 2415

Check2 BackColor = &H80000005&

Now Form1 would look like this

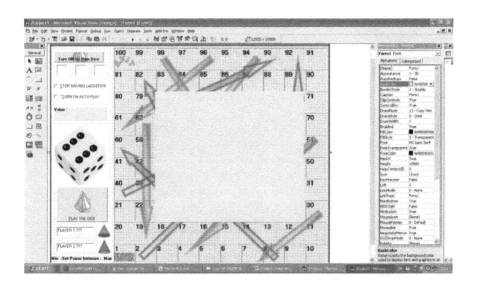

Now we shall add another control Horizontal Scroll Bar named

HScroll1 to Form1 with below properties:

HScroll1 Height = 255

HScroll1 LargeChange = 10

HScroll1 Left = 240

HScroll1 Max = 100

HScroll1 Min = 0

HScroll1 SmallChange = 1

HScroll1 Top = 9720

HScroll1 Value = 0

HScroll1 Width = 2295

Now Form1 would look like below:

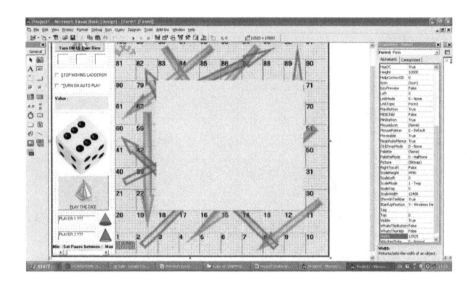

Now we shall add three Timers to Form1 Timer1, Timer2 and Timer3 like below

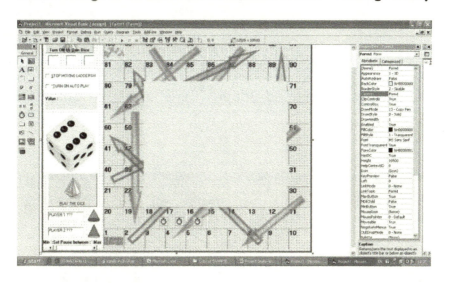

Set below properties to Timers

Timer1 Enabled = False

Timer1 Interval = 50

Timer1 Left = any value like 0 or 100 etc

Timer1 Top = any value like 0 or 100 etc

Timer2 Enabled = False

Timer2 Interval = 500

Timer2 Left = any value like 0 or 100 etc

Timer2 Top = any value like 0 or 100 etc

Timer3 Enabled = True

Timer3 Interval = 1000

Timer3 Left = any value like 0 or 100 etc

Timer3 Top = any value like 0 or 100 etc

Now we shall make two auto moving Ladders by adding array of 18 Shapes (Rectangle) named Shape1(0), Shape1(1)…Shape1(17) to Form1 like below.

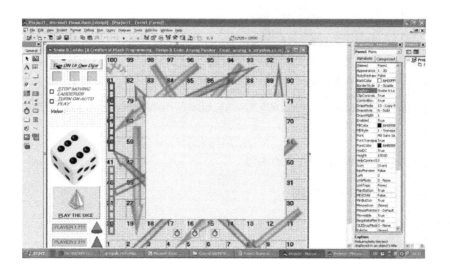

Red Ladder is made of 9 Rectangle Shapes named Shape1(0), Shape1(1)…Shape1(8) starting lower to upper. Blue Ladder is made of 9 Rectangle Shapes named Shape1(9), Shape1(10)…Shape1(17) starting upper to lower. Set below properties to Shape1(0) to Shape1(17)

Shape1(0) Backcolor = &H80000005&
Shape1(0) BackStyle = 0 – transparent

Shape1(0) BorderStyle = 1 – Solid

Shape1(0) BorderWidth = 5

Shape1(0) Height = 375

Shape1(0) Left = 2950

Shape1(0) Shape = 0- Rectangle

Shape1(0) Width = 255

Above properties will be same for Shape1(0) to Shape1(17)

Set BorderColor property for Shape1(0) to Shape1(8) as below

Shape1(0) BorderColor = &H000000FF&

Set BorderColor property for Shape1(9) to Shape1(17) as below

Shape1(0) BorderColor = &H00FF0000&

Top property of each Shape will be different. Set this property as below:

Shape1(0) Top = 8280

Shape1(1) Top = 7920

Shape1(2) Top = 7560

Shape1(3) Top = 7200

Shape1(4) Top = 6840

Shape1(5) Top = 6480

Shape1(6) Top = 6120

Shape1(7) Top = 5760

Shape1(8) Top = 5400

Shape1(9) Top = 1400

Shape1(10) Top = 1760

Shape1(11) Top = 2120

Shape1(12) Top = 2480

Shape1(13) Top = 2840

Shape1(14) Top = 3200

Shape1(15) Top = 3560

Shape1(16) Top = 3920

Shape1(17) Top = 4280

Look at below pictures for better understanding.

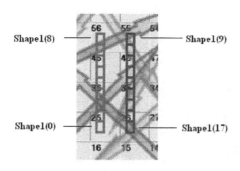

ABOVE TWO LADDERS ARE IN FACT SHAPE -0 RECTANGLE

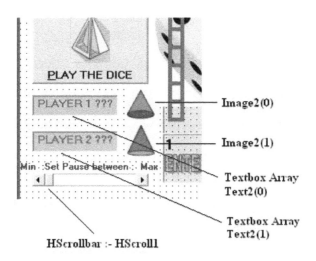

Now we have completed the designing part. Run the Program. It will look like below:

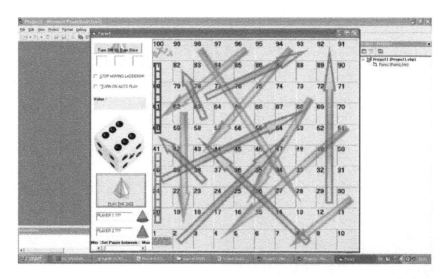

Step 7:

Now we shall complete the coding part. Entire code has been given below (from 'Snake & Ladder Code STARTS here to 'Snake & Ladder Code ENDS here). Go to your Visual Basic Project – Go to VIEW CODE

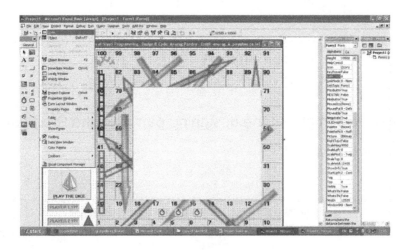

View Code Window would be blank like below.

Add given entire code in Visual Basic's Code window. Now it would look like this.

Please scroll down slowly and check if there are some lines colored in red? If yes then it may be due to long code line broken into multiple lines. Please make them one line and check.

Now SAVE the Project. Your Visual basic Snake & Ladder gaming Application is ready to perform. RUN and Check.

'Snake & Ladder Code STARTS here

```
Dim CNT, P(2), G, GS1L1, GS1L2, GS2L1, GS2L2, GG, I, J,
TURN, SIX, SEEDHI(13), SEEDHII(13), TURNN, NUMBERS(9, 9)
As Integer
Dim S As String
Private Sub Check1_Click()
If Check1.Value = 0 Then Timer2.Enabled = False
If Check1.Value = 1 Then
If Command1(1).Caption = "Turn OFF Ur &Own Dice" Then
Command1_Click (1)
End If
If Check1.Value = 1 And Command1(0).Enabled = True Then
Command1_Click (0)
End Sub
```

```vb
Private Sub Check2_Click()
If Check2.Value = 1 Then
Check2.Caption = "&MOVE THE LADDERS!!!"
Else
Check2.Caption = "&STOP MOVING LADDERS!!!"
End If
End Sub


Private Sub Command1_Click(Index As Integer)
If Index = 1 Then
    If Command1(1).Caption = "Turn ON Ur &Own Dice" Then
    Text1(0).Enabled = True
    Text1(0).Text = ""
    Text1(1).Text = ""
    Text1(2).Text = ""
    Text1(1).Enabled = False
    Text1(2).Enabled = False
    Check1.Value = 0
    Command1(1).Caption = "Turn OFF Ur &Own Dice"
    Text1(0).SetFocus
    Else
        Command1(1).Caption = "Turn ON Ur &Own Dice"
```

```
      Text1(0).Text = ""
      Text1(1).Text = ""
      Text1(2).Text = ""
      Text1(0).Enabled = False
      Text1(1).Enabled = False
      Text1(2).Enabled = False
   End If
Else
   If Command1(0).Caption = "PLAY AGAIN!" Then
   Label1(2).Visible = False
   Image2(0).Top = 8040
   Image2(0).Left = 2100
   Image2(1).Top = 8760
   Image2(1).Left = 2100
   P(0) = 0
   P(1) = 0
   I = 0
   J = 0
   G = 6
   GS1L1 = 101
   GS1L2 = 101
   GS2L1 = 101
```

```
    GS2L2 = 101

    GG = 0

    SIX = 0

    TURNN = 0

    Label1(1).Caption = ""

    TURN = 0
'Yellow & Green highlighted are one line/s
    Command1(0).Caption = Text2(TURN).Text & "! &PLAY THE
DICE!"
    Check1.Value = 0
    Else
    Timer1.Enabled = True
    Command1(0).Enabled = False
    End If
End If
End Sub


Private Sub Form_Load()
Label1(2).Visible = False
Image2(0).Top = 8040
Image2(0).Left = 2100
Image2(1).Top = 8760
```

```
Image2(1).Left = 2100
P(0) = 0
P(1) = 0
I = 0
J = 0
G = 6
GG = 0
    GS1L1 = 101
    GS1L2 = 101
    GS2L1 = 101
    GS2L2 = 101
SIX = 0
TURNN = 0
HScroll1.Value = 50
Label1(1).Caption = ""
TURN = 0
Command1(0).Caption = Text2(TURN).Text & "! &PLAY THE
DICE!"
SEEDHI(0) = 2
SEEDHI(1) = 8
SEEDHI(2) = 29
SEEDHI(3) = 38
```

SEEDHI(4) = 40

SEEDHI(5) = 63

SEEDHI(6) = 78

SEEDHI(7) = 54

SEEDHI(8) = 58

SEEDHI(9) = 92

SEEDHI(10) = 60

SEEDHI(11) = 68

SEEDHI(12) = 82

SEEDHI(13) = 93

SEEDHII(0) = 98

SEEDHII(1) = 94

SEEDHII(2) = 73

SEEDHII(3) = 62

SEEDHII(4) = 51

SEEDHII(5) = 30

SEEDHII(6) = 96

SEEDHII(7) = 28

SEEDHII(8) = 43

SEEDHII(9) = 25

SEEDHII(10) = 19

SEEDHII(11) = 4

```
SEEDHII(12) = 7
SEEDHII(13) = 61
Jj = 0
For I = 100 To 91 Step -1
NUMBERS(0, Jj) = I
Jj = Jj + 1
Next
Jj = 0
For I = 81 To 90
NUMBERS(1, Jj) = I
Jj = Jj + 1
Next
Jj = 0
For I = 80 To 71 Step -1
NUMBERS(2, Jj) = I
Jj = Jj + 1
Next
Jj = 0
For I = 61 To 70
NUMBERS(3, Jj) = I
Jj = Jj + 1
Next
```

```
Jj = 0
For I = 60 To 51 Step -1
NUMBERS(4, Jj) = I
Jj = Jj + 1
Next
Jj = 0
For I = 41 To 50
NUMBERS(5, Jj) = I
Jj = Jj + 1
Next
Jj = 0
For I = 40 To 31 Step -1
NUMBERS(6, Jj) = I
Jj = Jj + 1
Next
Jj = 0
For I = 21 To 30
NUMBERS(7, Jj) = I
Jj = Jj + 1
Next
Jj = 0
For I = 20 To 11 Step -1
```

```
NUMBERS(8, Jj) = I
Jj = Jj + 1
Next
Jj = 0
For I = 1 To 10
NUMBERS(9, Jj) = I
Jj = Jj + 1
Next
End Sub


Private Sub Text1_Change(Index As Integer)
If Index = 0 Then
    If Val(Text1(0).Text) = 6 Then
    Text1(1).Enabled = True
    Text1(0).Enabled = False
    End If
ElseIf Index = 1 Then
    If Val(Text1(1).Text) = 6 Then
    Text1(2).Enabled = True
    Text1(1).Enabled = False
    End If
Else
```

```vb
If Val(Text1(2).Text) = 6 Then
Text1(2).Enabled = False
End If
End If
If Val(Text1(Index).Text) > 0 Then
CNT = 20
I = Val(Text1(Index).Text)
Command1(0).Enabled = False
Timer1.Enabled = True
End If
End Sub


Private Sub Text1_KeyPress(Index As Integer, KeyAscii As Integer)
If KeyAscii < 49 Or KeyAscii > 54 Then
KeyAscii = 8
End If
End Sub


Private Sub Text2_Change(Index As Integer)
Command1(0).Caption = Text2(TURN).Text & " &PLAY THE
DICE!"
End Sub
```

```
Private Sub Text2_Click(Index As Integer)
Text2(Index).Text = ""
End Sub


Private Sub Timer1_Timer()
GG = 10
CNT = CNT + 1
If CNT < 21 Then
Randomize
I = Int((6) * Rnd + 1)
End If
For Jj = 1 To 6
If Jj = I Then
Image1(Jj - 1).Visible = True
Else
Image1(Jj - 1).Visible = False
End If
Next
If CNT > 15 Then
Timer1.Enabled = False
If P(TURN) = 0 And SIX = 0 And I <> 6 Then I = 0
```

```
If I = 6 Then
SIX = SIX + 6
    If CNT < 21 Then
    CNT = 0
    Timer2.Enabled = True
    End If
If SIX Mod 18 = 6 Then
Label1(1).Caption = "Value of (" & Text2(TURN).Text & "): 6"
ElseIf SIX Mod 18 = 12 Then
Label1(1).Caption = "Value of (" & Text2(TURN).Text & ") : 6 + 6"
Else
Label1(1).Caption = "Value of (" & Text2(TURN).Text & ") : 0"
If Command1(1).Caption = "Turn OFF Ur &Own Dice" Then
SIX = 0
Text1(0).Text = ""
Text1(1).Text = ""
Text1(2).Text = ""
Text1(1).Enabled = False
Text1(2).Enabled = False
Text1(0).Enabled = True
Text1(0).SetFocus
End If
```

```
        End If

        Exit Sub

        End If

        SIX = SIX Mod 18

If SIX > 0 Then

    If P(TURN) + I + SIX <= 100 Then

    SIX = SIX + I

    Label1(1).Caption = Label1(1).Caption & " + " & I

    Else

    SIX = 0

    End If

Else

    If P(TURN) + I <= 100 Then

    P(TURN) = P(TURN) + I

    Label1(1).Caption = "Value of (" & Text2(TURN).Text & ") : " & I

    Else

    I = 0

    Label1(1).Caption = "Value of (" & Text2(TURN).Text & ") : 0"

    End If

End If

CHAAL

GG = 0
```

```vb
CNT = 0
  If Command1(1).Caption = "Turn OFF Ur &Own Dice" Then
  Text1(0).Text = ""
  Text1(1).Text = ""
  Text1(2).Text = ""
  Text1(1).Enabled = False
  Text1(2).Enabled = False
  Text1(0).Enabled = True
  Text1(0).SetFocus
  End If
If Check1.Value = 1 And Command1(0).Enabled = True And
Command1(0).Caption <> "PLAY AGAIN!" Then
Timer2.Enabled = True
End If
Exit Sub
End If
End Sub
Function CHAAL()
Timer3.Enabled = False
If P(TURN) > 0 Or SIX > 0 Then
    While (SIX > 5)
    If Image2(TURN).Left < 2950 Then
```

```
Jj = 1
Else
Jj = 6
End If
Image2(TURN).Top = 9300 - Int((P(TURN) - 1 + Jj) / 10) *
1000


        If Int((P(TURN) - 1 + Jj) / 10) Mod 2 = 0 Then
        Image2(TURN).Left = 2950 + ((P(TURN) - 1 + Jj) Mod
10) * 970
        ElseIf (P(TURN) - 1 + Jj) = 20 Or (P(TURN) - 1 + Jj) = 40
Or (P(TURN) - 1 + Jj) = 60 Or (P(TURN) - 1 + Jj) = 80 Or (P(TURN)
- 1 + Jj) = 100 Then
        Image2(TURN).Left = 2950
        Else
        Image2(TURN).Left = 2950 + (10 - ((P(TURN) + Jj) Mod
10)) * 970
        End If
wait
If Image2(0).Left = Image2(1).Left And Image2(0).Top =
Image2(1).Top Then
Image2(1).Left = Image2(1).Left + 150
```

```
Image2(1).Top = Image2(1).Top + 150
End If
SIX = SIX - 6
If (P(TURN) + Jj) <= 100 Then P(TURN) = P(TURN) + Jj
For K = 0 To 6
    If P(TURN) = SEEDHI(K) Or P(TURN) = SEEDHII(K) Then
    If P(TURN) = SEEDHI(K) Then
    P(TURN) = SEEDHI(K + 7)
    TURNN = 1
    End If
    If P(TURN) = SEEDHII(K) Then P(TURN) = SEEDHII(K + 7)
    Image2(TURN).Top = 9300 - Int((P(TURN) - 1) / 10) * 1000
     If Int((P(TURN) - 1) / 10) Mod 2 = 0 Then
    Image2(TURN).Left = 2950 + ((P(TURN) - 1) Mod 10) * 970
    ElseIf P(TURN) = 20 Or P(TURN) = 40 Or P(TURN) = 60
Or P(TURN) = 80 Or P(TURN) = 100 Then
        Image2(TURN).Left = 2950
        Else
        Image2(TURN).Left = 2950 + (10 - ((P(TURN)) Mod 10))
* 970
        End If
    wait
```

```
    Exit For
    End If
    Next
Wend
If (P(TURN) + SIX) <= 100 Then P(TURN) = P(TURN) + SIX
SIX = 0
 Image2(TURN).Top = 9300 - Int((P(TURN) - 1) / 10) * 1000
If Int((P(TURN) - 1) / 10) Mod 2 = 0 Then
 Image2(TURN).Left = 2950 + ((P(TURN) - 1) Mod 10) * 970
 ElseIf P(TURN) = 20 Or P(TURN) = 40 Or P(TURN) = 60 Or
P(TURN) = 80 Or P(TURN) = 100 Then
    Image2(TURN).Left = 2950
    Else
    Image2(TURN).Left = 2950 + (10 - ((P(TURN)) Mod 10)) * 970
    End If
    For K = 0 To 6
        If P(TURN) = SEEDHI(K) Or P(TURN) = SEEDHII(K) Then
        If P(TURN) = SEEDHI(K) Then
        P(TURN) = SEEDHI(K + 7)
        TURNN = 1
        End If
        If P(TURN) = SEEDHII(K) Then P(TURN) = SEEDHII(K + 7)
```

```
wait
Image2(TURN).Top = 9300 - Int((P(TURN) - 1) / 10) * 1000
If Int((P(TURN) - 1) / 10) Mod 2 = 0 Then
Image2(TURN).Left = 2950 + ((P(TURN) - 1) Mod 10) * 970
ElseIf P(TURN) = 20 Or P(TURN) = 40 Or P(TURN) = 60 Or
P(TURN) = 80 Or P(TURN) = 100 Then
Image2(TURN).Left = 2950
Else
Image2(TURN).Left = 2950 + (10 - ((P(TURN)) Mod 10)) *
970
End If
Exit For
End If
Next
If Image2(0).Left = Image2(1).Left And Image2(0).Top =
Image2(1).Top Then
Image2(1).Left = Image2(1).Left + 150
Image2(1).Top = Image2(1).Top + 150
End If

End If
If P(TURN) = 100 Then
```

```
Label1(2).Caption = Text2(TURN).Text & " WON!!!"
Check1.Value = 0
Label1(2).Visible = True
Command1(0).Caption = "PLAY AGAIN!"
Command1(0).Enabled = True
Exit Function
End If
If TURNN = 0 Then
If TURN = 0 Then
    GS1L1 = 101
    GS1L2 = 101
TURN = 1
Else
    GS2L1 = 101
    GS2L2 = 101
TURN = 0
End If
Else
TURNN = 0
End If
Command1(0).Caption = Text2(TURN).Text & " &PLAY THE
DICE!"
```

```
Command1(0).Enabled = True

Command1(0).SetFocus

Timer3.Enabled = True

End Function

Function wait()

For ii = 0 To HScroll1.Value * 600000

Jj = Jj + 1

Next

End Function

Private Sub Timer2_Timer()

J = J + 1

If J >= Int(HScroll1.Value / 10) + 1 Then

J = 0

Timer2.Enabled = False

Command1_Click (0)

End If

End Sub


Private Sub Timer3_Timer()

If GG = 0 Then

G = G + 1

If G > 1 And Check2.Value = 0 Then
```

```
G = 0
Randomize
ii = Int((4221) * Rnd) + 1400
ii = 1400 + Int((ii - 1400) / 1000) * 1000
 For KK = 0 To 8
Shape1(KK).Top = ii + KK * 360
Next
Randomize
ii = Int((8551) * Rnd) + 2950
ii = 2950 + Int((ii - 2950) / 970) * 970
For KK = 0 To 8
Shape1(KK).Left = ii
Next

Randomize
ii = Int((4221) * Rnd) + 1400
ii = 1400 + Int((ii - 1400) / 1000) * 1000
For KK = 9 To 17
Shape1(KK).Top = ii + (KK - 9) * 360
Next
Randomize
ii = Int((8551) * Rnd) + 2950
```

```
ii = 2950 + Int((ii - 2950) / 970) * 970

If Shape1(0).Left = ii Then

If ii < (2950 + 9 * 970) Then

ii = ii + 970

Else

ii = ii - 970

End If

End If

For KK = 9 To 17

Shape1(KK).Left = ii

Next

End If

If P(0) = NUMBERS(Int((Shape1(0).Top - 1400) / 1000) + 1,

Int((Shape1(0).Left - 2950) / 970)) And GS1L1 <>

NUMBERS(Int((Shape1(0).Top - 1400) / 1000) + 4,

Int((Shape1(0).Left - 2950) / 970)) Then

GS1L1 = NUMBERS(Int((Shape1(0).Top - 1400) / 1000) + 1,

Int((Shape1(0).Left - 2950) / 970))

P(0) = NUMBERS(Int((Shape1(0).Top - 1400) / 1000) + 4,

Int((Shape1(0).Left - 2950) / 970))

ElseIf P(0) = NUMBERS(Int((Shape1(0).Top - 1400) / 1000) + 4,

Int((Shape1(0).Left - 2950) / 970)) And GS1L1 <>
```

```
NUMBERS(Int((Shape1(0).Top - 1400) / 1000) + 1,
Int((Shape1(0).Left - 2950) / 970)) Then
GS1L1 = NUMBERS(Int((Shape1(0).Top - 1400) / 1000) + 4,
Int((Shape1(0).Left - 2950) / 970))
P(0) = NUMBERS(Int((Shape1(0).Top - 1400) / 1000) + 1,
Int((Shape1(0).Left - 2950) / 970))
End If
If P(1) = NUMBERS(Int((Shape1(0).Top - 1400) / 1000) + 1,
Int((Shape1(0).Left - 2950) / 970)) And GS2L1 <>
NUMBERS(Int((Shape1(0).Top - 1400) / 1000) + 4,
Int((Shape1(0).Left - 2950) / 970)) Then
GS2L1 = NUMBERS(Int((Shape1(0).Top - 1400) / 1000) + 1,
Int((Shape1(0).Left - 2950) / 970))
P(1) = NUMBERS(Int((Shape1(0).Top - 1400) / 1000) + 4,
Int((Shape1(0).Left - 2950) / 970))
ElseIf P(1) = NUMBERS(Int((Shape1(0).Top - 1400) / 1000) + 4,
Int((Shape1(0).Left - 2950) / 970)) And GS2L1 <>
NUMBERS(Int((Shape1(0).Top - 1400) / 1000) + 1,
Int((Shape1(0).Left - 2950) / 970)) Then
GS2L1 = NUMBERS(Int((Shape1(0).Top - 1400) / 1000) + 4,
Int((Shape1(0).Left - 2950) / 970))
```

```
P(1) = NUMBERS(Int((Shape1(0).Top - 1400) / 1000) + 1,

Int((Shape1(0).Left - 2950) / 970))

End If

If P(0) = NUMBERS(Int((Shape1(9).Top - 1400) / 1000) + 1,

Int((Shape1(9).Left - 2950) / 970)) And GS1L2 <>

NUMBERS(Int((Shape1(9).Top - 1400) / 1000) + 4,

Int((Shape1(9).Left - 2950) / 970)) Then

GS1L2 = NUMBERS(Int((Shape1(9).Top - 1400) / 1000) + 1,

Int((Shape1(9).Left - 2950) / 970))

P(0) = NUMBERS(Int((Shape1(9).Top - 1400) / 1000) + 4,

Int((Shape1(9).Left - 2950) / 970))

ElseIf P(0) = NUMBERS(Int((Shape1(9).Top - 1400) / 1000) + 4,

Int((Shape1(9).Left - 2950) / 970)) And GS1L2 <>

NUMBERS(Int((Shape1(9).Top - 1400) / 1000) + 1,

Int((Shape1(9).Left - 2950) / 970)) Then

GS1L2 = NUMBERS(Int((Shape1(9).Top - 1400) / 1000) + 4,

Int((Shape1(9).Left - 2950) / 970))

P(0) = NUMBERS(Int((Shape1(9).Top - 1400) / 1000) + 1,

Int((Shape1(9).Left - 2950) / 970))

End If

If P(1) = NUMBERS(Int((Shape1(9).Top - 1400) / 1000) + 1,

Int((Shape1(9).Left - 2950) / 970)) And GS2L2 <>
```

```
NUMBERS(Int((Shape1(9).Top - 1400) / 1000) + 4,

Int((Shape1(9).Left - 2950) / 970)) Then

GS2L2 = NUMBERS(Int((Shape1(9).Top - 1400) / 1000) + 1,

Int((Shape1(9).Left - 2950) / 970))

P(1) = NUMBERS(Int((Shape1(9).Top - 1400) / 1000) + 4,

Int((Shape1(9).Left - 2950) / 970))

ElseIf P(1) = NUMBERS(Int((Shape1(9).Top - 1400) / 1000) + 4,

Int((Shape1(9).Left - 2950) / 970)) And GS2L2 <>

NUMBERS(Int((Shape1(9).Top - 1400) / 1000) + 1,

Int((Shape1(9).Left - 2950) / 970)) Then

GS2L2 = NUMBERS(Int((Shape1(9).Top - 1400) / 1000) + 4,

Int((Shape1(9).Left - 2950) / 970))

P(1) = NUMBERS(Int((Shape1(9).Top - 1400) / 1000) + 1,

Int((Shape1(9).Left - 2950) / 970))

End If

    If Image2(0).Left >= 2950 Then

    Image2(0).Top = 9300 - Int((P(0) - 1) / 10) * 1000

    If Int((P(0) - 1) / 10) Mod 2 = 0 Then

    Image2(0).Left = 2950 + ((P(0) - 1) Mod 10) * 970

    ElseIf P(0) = 20 Or P(0) = 40 Or P(0) = 60 Or P(0) = 80 Or

P(0) = 100 Then

    Image2(0).Left = 2950
```

```
Else
Image2(0).Left = 2950 + (10 - ((P(0)) Mod 10)) * 970
End If
For K = 0 To 6
    If P(0) = SEEDHI(K) Or P(0) = SEEDHII(K) Then
    If P(0) = SEEDHI(K) Then
    P(0) = SEEDHI(K + 7)
    End If
    If P(0) = SEEDHII(K) Then P(0) = SEEDHII(K + 7)
    wait
    Image2(0).Top = 9300 - Int((P(0) - 1) / 10) * 1000
    If Int((P(0) - 1) / 10) Mod 2 = 0 Then
    Image2(0).Left = 2950 + ((P(0) - 1) Mod 10) * 970
    ElseIf P(0) = 20 Or P(0) = 40 Or P(0) = 60 Or P(0) = 80 Or
P(0) = 100 Then
    Image2(0).Left = 2950
    Else
    Image2(0).Left = 2950 + (10 - ((P(0)) Mod 10)) * 970
    End If
    Exit For
    End If
Next
```

```
End If
If Image2(1).Left >= 2950 Then
Image2(1).Top = 9300 - Int((P(1) - 1) / 10) * 1000
If Int((P(1) - 1) / 10) Mod 2 = 0 Then
Image2(1).Left = 2950 + ((P(1) - 1) Mod 10) * 970
ElseIf P(1) = 20 Or P(1) = 40 Or P(1) = 60 Or P(1) = 80 Or
P(1) = 100 Then
Image2(1).Left = 2950
Else
Image2(1).Left = 2950 + (10 - ((P(1)) Mod 10)) * 970
End If

  For K = 0 To 6
    If P(1) = SEEDHI(K) Or P(1) = SEEDHII(K) Then
    If P(1) = SEEDHI(K) Then
    P(1) = SEEDHI(K + 7)
    End If
    If P(1) = SEEDHII(K) Then P(1) = SEEDHII(K + 7)
    wait
    Image2(1).Top = 9300 - Int((P(1) - 1) / 10) * 1000
    If Int((P(1) - 1) / 10) Mod 2 = 0 Then
    Image2(1).Left = 2950 + ((P(1) - 1) Mod 10) * 970
```

```
        ElseIf P(1) = 20 Or P(1) = 40 Or P(1) = 60 Or P(1) = 80 Or
P(1) = 100 Then
        Image2(1).Left = 2950
        Else
        Image2(1).Left = 2950 + (10 - ((P(1)) Mod 10)) * 970
        End If
        Exit For
        End If
    Next
    End If
    If Image2(0).Left = Image2(1).Left And Image2(0).Top =
Image2(1).Top Then
        Image2(1).Left = Image2(1).Left + 150
        Image2(1).Top = Image2(1).Top + 150
    End If
End If
End Sub
```

'Snake & Ladder Code ENDS here

Now Visual Basic based Snake & Ladder gaming Application is
ready. You can also make EXE file of this project.

Click on FILE MENU and CLICK on Make Project1.exe Submenu as shown below.

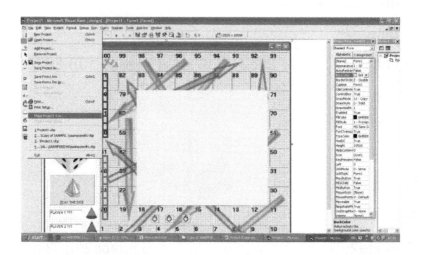

Choose Location and give any Name to the exe file and then Click on OK.

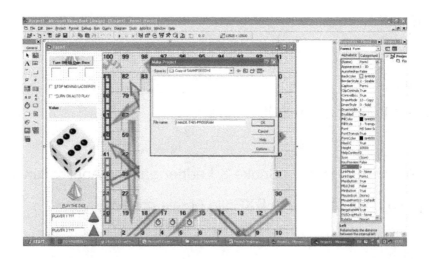

Now Exe file of Snake & Ladder is ready and anyone can play this game on any Windows based Computer.

Project accomplished!

Date: 16-08-2020

About the Author

Anurag S Pandey

Anurag S Pandey aged 41 years lives in Bhubaneswar, India. He is doing job in private sector. But his passion is Writing and Computer Programming.

Email: anurag_k_p@yahoo.co.in

anuragspandey@gmail.com

Face book Page:

https://www.facebook.com/HalfCoockedThoughts/?ref=bookmarks

Thanks…